D0323820

Meatloaf

· · · · · · · · · · · · · · · ·

Meatloaf

42 Recipes—from Down-Home Classics to New Variations

Sharon Moore

Illustrations by Sally Sturman

GRAMERCY BOOKS
NEW YORK

To my mother,
Avis Marie Stewart Freeman,
and to
David and Ian
. . . .

Copyright © 1991 by Lamp Post Press
Illustrations copyright © 1991 by Sally Sturman

All rights reserved under International and Pan-American
Copyright Conventions.

No part of this book may be reproduced or transmitted in any form
or by any means, electronic or mechanical, including photocopying,
recording or by any information storage and retrieval system, without
permission in writing from the publisher.

This 2003 edition published by Gramercy Books, an imprint of Random
House Value Publishing, a division of Random House Inc., New York,
by arrangement with Clarkson Potter/Publishers, New York.

Gramercy Books is a registered trademark and the colophon is a
trademark of Random House Inc.

Printed in the United States of America.

Design by Renato Stanisic

Random House
New York • Toronto • London • Sydney • Auckland
www.randomhouse.com

A catalog record for this title is available from the Library of
Congress.

ISBN: 0-517-22231-0

9 8 7 6 5 4 3 2 1

Contents

. . . .

Introduction

Homey, hearty, comforting, and reliable, good old-fashioned meatloaf like Mother used to make is today more popular than ever.

Contemporary palates are tiring of trendy cuisines and fast food, and food lovers are turning to "postmodern" down-home cookery. Further, meat itself is enjoying something of a renaissance. Beef and chicken are leaner than ever. Nutritionists are speaking out about meat's value as a source of complete protein, iron, calcium, and other minerals. And what better way to make the most of meat's nutrients and its wonderful taste than to blend it with grains and vegetables in a meatloaf! The leanest cuts can be turned into rich, juicy loaves without any additional fat. If you're counting cholesterol, red meat can be partially or entirely replaced with low-cholesterol poultry (see page 4).

Budget crunching is another reason to welcome the return of the meatloaf. Many cooks are discovering "meatloaf economics," stretching their food dollars by shrinking their meat expenditures. And as you'll see on page 84, creating a meatloaf can be considered the art of using leftovers—avoiding waste while giving the chef a chance to go a little wild and show what he or she can do.

Finally, meatloaf is a favorite dish because it need never be boring. In this book you'll find a wide variety . . . meatloaves to make in a minute, meatloaves to impress your boss, meatloaves to stretch your budget, and meatloaves just to make you feel warm and loved. There are ethnic and regional loaves,

loaves with unexpected ingredients, loaves little and big.

So here's a tribute to everyone's mom and her culinary ambassador, the meatloaf!

I N G R E D I E N T S

The tastiness of a meatloaf is inherent in the quality of its ingredients. Don't expect salt or spices to mask the poor flavor of overcooked vegetables or inferior meat, or the firmness of the meat to make up for the flabbiness of white bread crumbs.

Meatloaf ingredients can be broken down into five basic "food groups." Within each is a variety of possibilities. A rule of thumb is, "If you can eat it, you can put it in a meatloaf."

Meat: *Ground beef from cuts such as sirloin and round have less fat and a more delicate taste than chuck, and equal portions of beef, pork, and veal (or half beef and one-quarter each of pork and veal) create a more interesting flavor than beef alone. Veal makes a subtle, sophisticated loaf. Chicken and turkey make delectable loaves with pleasing textures.*

The "meat" can also be fish; grated cheddar, Swiss, Gruyère, mozzarella, Parmesan, or other cheese; nuts; or legumes combined to form complete proteins. Use a firm-fleshed fish; don't overpower it with other flavors, and shorten the cooking time. Zip up cheese loaves with cayenne pepper or other hot spices; add mushrooms and nuts for textural interest. Cooked dried beans can be combined with cornmeal or cornbread or cooked rice to make up part or all of the "meat" of a loaf.

Bread crumbs: *Soft white bread creates a delicate, if flabby meatloaf. Whole wheat bread stands up to hearty meat flavors* better. Packaged bread crumbs are usually made from white bread and are often high in sodium. Dry or toasted crumbs preclude a soggy loaf, while crumbs soaked in milk, wine, or stock add smoothness and extra flavor. Rye bread provides a robust flavor. Cornbread crumbs are delicious but don't soak up as much of the liquid in cooking as other kinds of bread.

Grains, such as cooked rice or bulgur, and lentils or pasta can substitute for much of the bread crumbs, but use them with at least ¼ cup of dry bread crumbs or you'll get a heavy, wet loaf. Bran, wheat germ, crumbled crackers, cornflakes and other breakfast cereals can take the place of bread crumbs.

Binding: An egg traditionally is used to hold a meatloaf together. Use 2 eggs for a large loaf that incorporates more than 2 pounds of ground meat. Or use 2 or more eggs for a delicate custardy texture. Cream and sour cream also help hold a loaf together.

Moistener: Bread that has been soaked in milk, wine, or stock usually provides enough liquid for a meatloaf. Cooked onions, peppers, mushrooms, and tomatoes also help keep a loaf moist. If you use dry bread crumbs or raw vegetables that require a longer cooking time, add milk, chicken or beef stock, wine, or water to keep the loaf from drying out.

Another usual method for keeping a loaf moist is to cover the top with bacon strips or ketchup. I rarely use bacon because of the added fat and nitrates (although the taste is delicious); I prefer to substitute fresh tomato sauce for ketchup to cut down on salt and sugar. Basting the loaf with ¼ cup of liquid before the last 15 minutes of baking is an excellent method for ensuring a moist, tender loaf, but it does add a flavor of its own—so make sure the flavor of the basting liquid is compatible with the loaf's ingredients.

Flavorings: Everything from oregano to mustard to soy sauce can be used to add zest to a meatloaf. The recipes in this book call on a variety of ingredients for flavor interest, such as watercress, raisins, chili powder, and fresh corn. Meatloaves, like most other meat dishes, are enhanced by the tastes of onions, garlic, celery, peppers, green herbs, lemon juice, wine, and sherry. Complex flavors take a while to develop, so it's best to let cooked meatloaf sit for 10 to 15 minutes before serving.

ALTERNATIVE INGREDIENTS

Meatloaf can be made to fit within the restrictions of any low-fat, low-cholesterol, low-calorie, low-salt, high-fiber diet by substituting the right ingredients for the no-nos, and in the right proportions. Cut down on the amount of red meat and increase the (high-fiber) bread crumbs. Use fish or grated hard, low-fat cheese in place of all or part of the red meat. Use cottage cheese or tofu in combination with any of the meats, poultry, fish, or hard cheeses listed here. Substitute shredded carrots and other vegetables for some of the meat. Use small amounts of polyunsaturated or monounsaturated oils to sauté vegetables. Here are some substitutes you can use in the recipes in this book.

For ground beef or pork, use chicken; turkey; veal; fish, fresh or canned, flaked; low-fat cheese, such as Alpine Lace or Premonde brands, shredded; cottage or pot cheese (press out excess moisture by wrapping in paper towels and then weighting for several hours); tofu (press out excess moisture as above and finely chop).

For bread or bread crumbs, use high-fiber, low-fat bread and crackers; bran (wheat, oat, or rice); high-fiber breakfast cereal; ground millet, soy grits, cornbread; cooked rice, bulgur, pasta, potatoes, lentils, barley, dried beans and peas; wheat germ.

For eggs, use 2 egg whites for each whole egg.

For liquids, use low-fat or skim milk; low-fat yogurt (for sour cream and cream); defatted homemade chicken, beef, or veal stock (commercial stocks and broths are high in added salt); fish stock (avoid bottled clam juice because of its high sodium content); dry white or red table wine; liquid from cooking vegetables, including potatoes.

For flavorings, use all herbs and spices (hot spicy flavors often appeal to dieters); grated lemon and other citrus peel; lemon juice; salt substitutes (in place of salty flavorings); soy sauce in limited amounts.

MAKING A PERFECT MEATLOAF

To blend the ingredients for meatloaf, start by beating the egg or eggs and blending in other liquid ingredients, then the herbs and flavorings. Mix in the bread crumbs, meat, and other solid ingredients.

The best way to mix a meatloaf is with your hands, squeezing the mixture through your fingers by handfuls. (You can do this with just one hand, keeping the other clean in case the phone rings.) Squeezing blends the flavorings throughout the ground meat. If you're in a hurry, skip the preliminary steps outlined above, plump everything into a mixing bowl (including the egg, unbeaten), and squeeze away until you have a homogenous mixture. This method is usually adequate to blend ingredients for most loaves.

Meatloaf chefs are of two minds about shaping the loaf. A meatloaf patted into an oval shape and baked in a pan larger than the loaf will be firmer than one baked in a loaf pan. (To keep the loaf from reabsorbing the fat it emits during cooking, place it on a rack in the baking pan.)

Other cooks, including myself, find that a meatloaf stays juicier and retains more of its flavor (and proteins) if it is pressed into a loaf pan. Although the fat (part of the brown foam that sometimes accumulates when meat is cooked) is also retained, you shouldn't be too concerned about excess fat if you use low-fat ingredients.

If you use a loaf pan, coat the sides and bottom with oil or butter to prevent the loaf from sticking. A light coating is all that is needed for most loaves. Or use a nonstick loaf pan.

The standard 9 x 5 x 3-inch loaf pan is a fine size for all loaves, but smaller loaves (those containing less than 1½ pounds of meat) will come out looking a bit squat and may be dry. Use an 8½ x 4½ x 2½-inch pan for these.

Most loaves are baked in a moderate oven—350° to 375°F. —for even cooking throughout. Delicate ingredients cook faster; raw ingredients, such as vegetables, blended into the loaf take longer. Test a loaf for doneness by pressing down on the top; if it springs back or feels firm, it is probably done.

Let the finished loaf rest in the pan for 10 to 15 minutes to allow the flavors to develop. Some of the more complexly flavored loaves taste even better the day after cooking, and most are delectable cold. Slice leftover meatloaf for sandwiches; place slices on lettuce leaves and serve as a first course; or cut them into cubes and serve with toothpicks (perhaps with a dipping sauce) as hors d'oeuvres.

Sauces add a finishing touch to a meatloaf presentation. Make sure your loaf-sauce combination is a heavenly marriage; neither partner should overpower the other. You can serve rich sauces, such as Raisin or Figgy, on the side, like condiments. Decorate the loaf or individual slices creatively with colorful Tomato Sauce. Or pour some of the sauce onto a serving plate, top with a slice of meatloaf, and garnish for an elegant effect. For a modern touch, serve two sauces, such as Figgy and Sorrel, or Tomato Sauce and sour cream, or a plum wine sauce and a cream sauce, one on either side of each meatloaf serving.

Garnish your meatloaf or serving slices generously to enhance their appeal. If the finished loaf lacks color, enliven it with sprigs of parsley or other green herbs; strips of red, green, orange, or yellow pepper; tomato wedges; spears of chives; or slivers of leek. Or take your garnishing cue from the loaf's ingredients: a loaf with lemon flavoring deserves a little curl of lemon peel; a fan of celery sliced on the diagonal signals the presence of the same vegetable in the dish; little chunks of steamed corn on the cob ornament a cornbread loaf. Key in Oriental flavors with festoons of bean sprouts or coriander leaves. Pickles, olives, marinated or broiled stuffed mushrooms, apple slices, orange segments, baby vegetables, and nuts of all kinds will set off the appearance and the taste of the meatloaf you so lovingly prepared.

Classic
Meatloaf

Granny's Meatloaf

....

This is a simple loaf with old-fashioned goodness, just like the ones Grandma used to make.

SERVES 6

   1 pound ground beef

  ½ pound ground veal

  ½ pound ground pork

   2 large eggs

  ½ cup fine bread crumbs

  ¾ cup chopped parsley

  ½ teaspoon dried oregano

  ½ teaspoon dried basil

  ¼ cup coarsely chopped green pepper (optional)

1½ teaspoons salt

  ½ teaspoon freshly ground black pepper

3–4 strips bacon

Preheat the oven to 350°F.

Place all ingredients except the bacon in a bowl. Briefly blend well and form into a loaf. Place the loaf on a rack in a 10-inch baking pan and cover with the bacon slices.

Bake for 1½ hours, until the loaf is firm and the bacon is browned. Serve with Mushroom Sauce (page 98) or Tomato Sauce (page 96).

Basic Meatloaf

....

Earthy and elemental, this recipe includes the essential vegetables, herbs, and spices associated with classic meat cookery.

S E R V E S 6 T O 8

½ cup fresh bread crumbs
¼ cup milk
1 pound ground beef
½ pound ground pork shoulder
½ pound veal shoulder, ground twice
1 small onion, grated
1 carrot, finely shredded
2 garlic cloves, minced
1 teaspoon salt
1 teaspoon prepared mustard, preferably Dijon
½ teaspoon freshly ground black pepper
½ teaspoon dried thyme
   Pinch nutmeg
2 large eggs, lightly beaten
6 strips bacon

Preheat the oven to 350°F.

Soak the bread crumbs in the milk until soft. Pour off any excess milk.

Combine the meats, onion, carrot, and seasonings, and blend well. Mix in the eggs and bread crumbs, combining thoroughly.

Spread 4 strips of bacon in a shallow 8-inch baking pan. Form the meat mixture into a firm loaf and place on top of the bacon. Place the remaining bacon across the top of the loaf.

Bake for about 1 hour, or until firm and browned, basting several times with the pan juices. Serve warm or cold.

Note: To serve the meatloaf cold, remove from the pan, wrap it tightly in foil, place a heavy pan or other weight on top, and let sit until the loaf has cooled and is firm.

Pickled Ham Loaf

....

Down-home and delicious, this loaf enabled Grandma to show off the quality of her pickling spice recipe (and to use up the leftover pickle juice, too). Country-cured ham lends the best flavor to this dish.

SERVES 6 TO 8

4 slices bread, preferably whole wheat

1 cup milk

2 large eggs

1 teaspoon dried savory, crumbled
   Salt and freshly ground pepper to taste

1 cup finely chopped onion

2 garlic cloves, minced

2 pounds ground pork

1 pound ground smoked ham

1 cup juice from a jar of sweet pickles, such as bread-and-
   butter pickles, gherkins, or cornichons

Preheat the oven to 350°F.

Soak the bread in the milk. Beat the eggs and blend in the seasonings, then add the onion and garlic. Mix in the pork, ham, and bread, and press the mixture into an oiled 9 x 5 x 3-inch loaf pan.

Bake for 45 minutes. Pour the pickle juice over the loaf and bake another 15 to 20 minutes, until most of the liquid has been absorbed. Let the loaf stand 10 to 15 minutes before serving.

Country-Style Meatloaf

....

What's special about this loaf is the farm flavoring of salt pork.

SERVES 6 TO 8

1 pound ground beef

1 pound ground pork

1 pound ground veal

2 garlic cloves, minced

1 large onion, chopped

1 teaspoon salt

2 large eggs, lightly beaten

1 teaspoon freshly ground black pepper

1 bay leaf

½ teaspoon dried thyme

½ teaspoon dried tarragon

1 green pepper, chopped

½ cup fine dry bread crumbs

¼ pound salt pork, thinly sliced

Preheat the oven to 325°F.

Combine all ingredients except the salt pork. Form into a firm loaf.

Lay some of the salt pork slices on the bottom of a 9 x 5 x 3-inch loaf pan and place the loaf on top. Arrange the remaining slices of salt pork over the loaf.

Bake for 2 hours, until the loaf is firm and the salt pork browned, basting occasionally.

Giacomo's Meatloaf

....

This delicious loaf was developed by Jack Ubaldi, founder of
the Florence Meat Market in Greenwich Village, New York; Cor-
don Bleu chef; and lecturer at the New School of Culinary Arts
in New York City.

SERVES 6

1½ slices good-quality white bread, untrimmed, crumbled
½ cup milk
1 pound fresh spinach
1 pound ground chuck
½ pound ground pork
½ pound ground veal
1 large egg, lightly beaten
2 tablespoons grated Parmesan cheese
  Salt and freshly ground black pepper to taste
  Olive oil

Preheat the oven to 350°F.

Soak the crumbled bread in the milk until soft. Squeeze
out the excess milk.

Rinse the spinach thoroughly and remove the tough
stems. Place in a large pot with just the water that clings to
the leaves. Cook over medium heat for about 5 minutes,
stirring once or twice. Drain in a colander and press out the
excess moisture with the back of a wooden spoon. Chop finely.

Thoroughly mix all ingredients except the oil and shape
into a loaf.

Meatloaf

Place in a 10-inch baking pan or in a small casserole. You may wish to surround the loaf with potatoes, mushrooms, and/or whole small onions. Spread a little olive oil over the top of the loaf.

Bake for 1 hour, until firm.

Variations: Mix ingredients as above, reserving spinach. Pat the meatloaf into a rectangle 9 inches wide; spread chopped spinach to within 1 inch of the edges and roll up like a jelly roll. Bake as directed.

Or open up the center of the meatloaf by pressing a finger halfway in down the length of the loaf. Press the chopped spinach into the center as a filling. Shape into a loaf again and bake as above.

Meatloaf
Bourguignonne

....

The classic taste of beef Burgundy in a quick-and-easy meatloaf. This dish can be the centerpiece of a company dinner,
served with roasted potatoes or buttered noodles and a good
red wine. Be sure to use good wine in the meatloaf as well; it
really makes a difference!

SERVES 6 TO 8

2 tablespoons vegetable oil

2 cups chopped onions

1 pound fresh mushrooms, diced

½ cup dry red wine, preferably Burgundy

2 large eggs

½ cup milk

1½ teaspoons dried thyme

1 teaspoon dried savory

½ teaspoon nutmeg

Salt and freshly ground black pepper to taste

2 pounds ground sirloin

3 cups fine bread crumbs

Preheat the oven to 350°F.

Heat the oil over medium heat and sauté the onions
briefly, until translucent. Add the mushrooms and sauté a
few minutes. Add the wine and raise the heat to high; simmer

briskly until most of the liquid is absorbed (about 5 minutes). Cool slightly.

Beat the eggs in a mixing bowl; blend in the milk and seasonings. Blend in the sirloin and bread crumbs. Add the mushroom mixture and mix well. Press into a buttered or oiled 9 x 5 x 3-inch loaf pan.

Bake for 1 hour, until firm. Let the loaf stand 15 minutes before serving.

Susie's Microwave Meatloaf

....

My sister Susie, who is the microwave guru in our family, passed along this marvelous recipe to me, and it was an instant hit with my family. It's a snap to make and so good you'd think it took hours to prepare.

SERVES 4 TO 6

1 large egg
¼ cup milk
1 cup uncooked oatmeal (noninstant)
1½ pounds ground beef
1 cup chopped onion
1 teaspoon dried thyme
2 tablespoons Dijon mustard
½ cup chopped parsley
Salt and freshly ground black pepper to taste
½ cup Tomato Sauce (page 96) (optional)

Beat the egg and add the milk. Soak the oatmeal in this mixture for 30 minutes.

Add the remaining ingredients except the Tomato Sauce and mix well. Form into a round loaf or a rectangular loaf with uniformly thick corners, and place in an 8-inch glass or other microwave baking pan large enough to prevent the loaf from touching the sides. Cover the top of the loaf with Tomato Sauce if using.

Bake on full/high setting for 16–20 minutes, rotating the pan every 7 minutes if necessary. Let the loaf stand 5 minutes before serving.

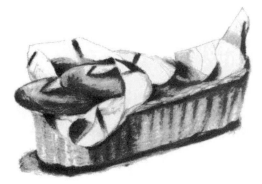

Company
Meatloaf

Sherried Ham Loaf

....

Festive and savory, this loaf is rich enough for the fanciest company dinner. Try it with Raisin Sauce (page 102) or with your favorite mustard sauce, fruit conserve, or corn relish.

SERVES 6 TO 8

    2 large eggs
  ½ cup sherry
    2 tablespoons Dijon mustard
  ¼ cup dark brown sugar, firmly packed
    1 teaspoon dried sage, crumbled
      Salt and freshly ground black pepper to taste
  ½ teaspoon grated nutmeg
    2 cups fine dry bread crumbs
    1 pound ground lean pork
    1 pound ground smoked ham

Preheat the oven to 350°F.

Beat the eggs and blend in the sherry and mustard. Add the brown sugar and stir to dissolve; stir in the seasonings. Blend in the bread crumbs, pork, and ham. Press into an oiled 9 x 5 x 3-inch loaf pan.

Bake for 1 hour, until firm.

Chicken Loaf
Pain de Poule

....

This elegant dish for health-conscious guests forgoes red meat entirely yet tastes as subtly rich as a pâté. It makes an attractive presentation served with rich green Watercress Sauce and rice or noodles. Delicious cold, the loaf also makes excellent sandwiches.

SERVES 6 TO 8

    2 pounds skinless, boneless chicken breasts
    1 large egg
1½ cups heavy cream
    ½ cup finely chopped shallots
    1 cup diced fresh mushrooms
    2 cups fine bread crumbs
1½ teaspoons dried tarragon
1½ teaspoons dried thyme
    ¼ teaspoon grated nutmeg
      Salt and freshly ground white pepper to taste
    ½ cup chopped almonds or cashews

Preheat the oven to 350°F.

Cut the chicken into 2-inch cubes and process them in a food processor with the egg and cream, scraping down the sides of the bowl as necessary. (The chicken may have to be processed in two or three batches.)

Place the chicken mixture in a mixing bowl and add the remaining ingredients. Blend well. Place in a buttered 9 x 5 x 3-inch loaf pan, top with a piece of buttered wax paper (buttered side down), and cover tightly with aluminum foil. Set the loaf pan in a larger pan filled with enough boiling water to come halfway up the sides of the loaf pan.

Bake for 1½ hours, until firm. Let the loaf stand 10 minutes before unmolding. Serve with Watercress Sauce (page 100), Mushroom Sauce (page 98), Tomato Sauce (page 96), or your favorite hollandaise sauce.

Company Meatloaf

Blue Ribbon Loaf

....

A *rolled loaf filled with blue cheese, this makes a savory first course served in slices on lettuce leaves and accompanied by a sturdy red wine. If there happens to be any left over, it's delicious cold the next day, on French bread.*

SERVES 6 TO 8

2 large eggs

1 tablespoon Dijon mustard

¼ cup port

  Salt (if desired) and freshly ground black pepper to taste

1 pound ground veal

1 pound ground lean pork

3 cups fine dry bread crumbs

1 cup finely chopped onion

¼ pound blue cheese, crumbled

  Red grapes (optional)

Preheat the oven to 350°F.

Beat the eggs in a mixing bowl; blend in the mustard and port. Stir in the salt and pepper (salt may not be necessary unless using processed blue cheese.) Work in the veal, pork, bread crumbs, and onion, and blend thoroughly.

Place the mixture on a 24-inch-long piece of wax paper and press it into a 9 x 16-inch rectangle. Sprinkle the blue cheese evenly over the top, leaving a margin of 1½ inches on all sides. Carefully roll up the rectangle like a jelly roll, sealing the outside seam and ends by pressing down firmly.

Transfer the roll to a buttered or oiled 9 x 5 x 3-inch loaf pan by picking it up in the wax paper and inverting it.

Bake for 45 minutes to 1 hour, until firm. Garnish with red grapes, if desired.

British Beef Braid

....

Something different from across the Atlantic, this dish is as cozy as an English fireside and special enough for high tea. The "bread" portion of the loaf forms a shell for the meat filling. Serve garnished with English garden flowers, like marigolds and nasturtiums.

SERVES 4 TO 6

Bread
- 1 tablespoon (1 envelope) yeast
- 2 tablespoons sugar
- 2 cups lukewarm water
- 1 large egg
- 2 teaspoons salt
- 2 tablespoons vegetable oil or melted unsalted butter
- 3 cups all-purpose flour, plus flour for rolling dough
- 1 large egg beaten with 1 tablespoon water for glaze

Meat Filling
- 1 medium leek
- 1 pound ground lean beef
- 1 teaspoon curry powder
- 2 tablespoons vegetable oil
- 1 Granny Smith or other tart apple, unpeeled, cored, and coarsely chopped
- ¼ pound fresh mushrooms, sliced

2 tablespoons all-purpose or unbleached white flour
   Salt and freshly ground black pepper to taste
1 cup beef stock
¼ cup raisins

To prepare the bread, sprinkle the yeast and sugar over the water and let stand 10 minutes to "proof" (bubble up). Place in a mixing bowl, add the egg, salt, and oil, and begin blending in the flour, a cup at a time, beating with a wooden spoon until smooth. Cover the bowl with a damp cloth and let rise in a warm place away from drafts for about 1 hour.

Turn the dough out on a floured surface and knead about fifty times, giving the dough a quarter turn each time, until a smooth, elastic ball is produced. Place the dough in a clean oiled bowl, cover with a damp cloth, and let rise in a warm place about 1 hour.

When the dough has doubled in size, punch it down, recover, and let it stand another hour, or until it has doubled in size.

Meanwhile, trim the ends of the leek and cut it in half lengthwise. Separate the leaves and rinse well under running water. Pat dry and cut into ½-inch slices.

Brown the beef with the curry powder in a skillet over medium-high heat. Remove with a slotted spoon. Heat 1 tablespoon of the oil in the skillet, and sauté the leek, apple, and mushrooms just until tender. Remove with a slotted spoon.

Heat the remaining oil in the skillet, add the flour, and stir with a wire whisk until blended. Whisk in the salt, pepper, and stock, and stir until the mixture boils and thickens. Blend the beef, leek mixture, and raisins into the sauce. Cool slightly.

To assemble the loaf, punch down the dough. On a floured work surface, roll the dough out into a rectangle about 12 inches wide and ½ inch thick. Spread the beef filling down the center of the dough, from top to bottom, leaving 4 inches of the dough uncovered on each side. Make diagonal cuts on each side about 1 inch apart, from the filling to the edge of the dough. Alternating sides, fold the strips of dough over the filling, overlapping them to form a braid. Stretch the strips slightly as you fold and press them firmly into place to make a compact loaf. Place the loaf on a greased (or nonstick) baking sheet and let rise 20 minutes.

Brush the loaf with the egg glaze and bake for 1 hour, or until golden brown. Let stand 15 minutes before serving.

Meatloaf

Lemon Veal Loaf

....

Delicate and soothing, this lemon-scented loaf is perfect for summer entertaining. Serve with a green salad and a California chardonnay.

SERVES 6 TO 8

1 cup finely chopped onion

¾ cup diced celery

2 tablespoons (¼ stick) unsalted butter

1 large egg

½ teaspoon salt

Grated zest of 1 lemon

¼ teaspoon cayenne pepper, or to taste

¾ cup sour cream

2 pounds ground veal

2½ cups fine dry bread crumbs

Preheat the oven to 350°F.

Sauté the onion and celery in the butter until translucent; cool slightly.

Beat the egg lightly in a mixing bowl, then blend in the salt, lemon zest, cayenne pepper, and sour cream. Work in the veal and bread crumbs; add the onion-celery mixture and blend thoroughly. Press into a buttered 9 x 5 x 3-inch loaf pan.

Bake for 45 minutes to 1 hour, or until firm. Let stand 10 minutes before serving. Garnish with half slices of lemon, the peel carved back halfway around the slice and curled under.

Veal Loaf Nouvelle

....

Here's a special loaf that's healthy, too. For an attractive presentation, garnish it with finely shredded spears of leek greens, enoki mushrooms, and carved slices of blanched or raw carrot and turnip. Serve with brown rice and lightly stir-fried vegetables and soy sauce or a soy sauce–sesame oil vinaigrette on the side.

SERVES 4 TO 6

1 medium leek

½ pound shiitake mushrooms, preferably fresh or about
    8 to 10 dried

1 tablespoon unsalted butter

1 tablespoon vegetable oil

1 large egg

2 tablespoons soy sauce, preferably tamari

2 tablespoons mirin (Japanese sweet wine) or sherry
    Salt and freshly ground black pepper to taste

2 pounds ground veal

1½ cups fine dry bread crumbs

Preheat the oven to 350°F.

Trim the ends of the leek and slice it into thin rings; rinse well and pat dry. Wash the fresh mushrooms, pat dry, trim the stems, and cut the mushrooms into strips, if large, or quarters, if small. (If using dried mushrooms, soak them in hot water about 30 minutes, or until softened; pat dry, remove stems, and cut as above.)

Heat the butter and oil in a skillet until the butter foams. Add the mushrooms and sauté a few minutes; add the leek rings and sauté 1 or 2 minutes, until wilted. Cool slightly.

Beat the egg in a mixing bowl. Blend in the flavorings. Add the veal and bread crumbs, and mix well.

Decorate the bottom of a buttered or oiled 9 x 5 x 3-inch loaf pan with about one-fourth of the leek rings and mushroom slices or quarters.

Add the remaining leek rings and mushrooms to the veal mixture and blend in thoroughly. Press the mixture into the loaf pan.

Bake for 45 minutes to 1 hour, until firm. Let the loaf stand about 10 minutes, then unmold onto a platter.

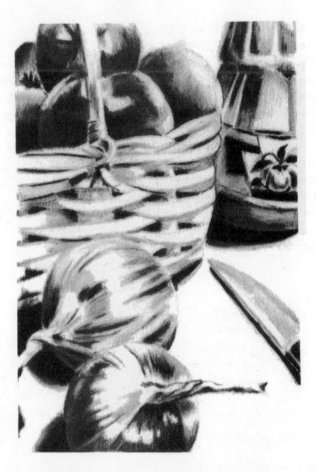

Regional
Meatloaf

Tex-Mex Meatloaf

....

Chili you can slice! This makes a great buffet dish for your next hoedown. You can spice it up with your favorite hot sauce for a "five alarm" sensation.

SERVES 6 TO 8

1 large egg

1 tablespoon molasses

2 tablespoons tomato paste

1 tablespoon Dijon mustard

¼ teaspoon Worcestershire sauce

1 teaspoon chili powder, or to taste

Hot sauce to taste

1 teaspoon dried thyme

Salt and freshly ground black pepper to taste

1½ pounds ground beef

½ cup fresh bread crumbs

1 cup finely chopped onion

1 garlic clove, minced

1 carrot, grated

½ cup cooked kidney beans, drained and patted dry

Preheat the oven to 350°F.

In a mixing bowl, beat the egg and blend in the molasses, tomato paste, mustard, and Worcestershire sauce until thoroughly combined. Blend in the chili powder, hot sauce, thyme, salt, and pepper. Mix in the ground beef, bread crumbs, onion, garlic, and carrot, and blend well. Carefully mix in the kidney beans to avoid mashing them.

Place the mixture in an oiled 9 x 5 x 3-inch loaf pan and press down lightly.

Bake for 45 minutes to 1 hour, until firm and browned.

California Sushi Loaf

....

This colorful loaf adds a Japanese accent to the fresh flavors of the Far West's fields and waters. Cut into small slices for appetizers, or serve for lunch with a green salad that has a sesame oil dressing.

SERVES 6 TO 8

1 cup short-grain brown rice

1 teaspoon salt

1 (4-inch) piece kombu seaweed, available in Oriental stores (optional)

4 teaspoons sugar, or to taste

3 tablespoons rice wine or cider vinegar

½ pound large shrimp

1 garlic clove, minced

½ dried Oriental hot pepper pod, seeds removed

1 tablespoon unsalted butter

½ pound crab meat, preferably lump

1 tablespoon mirin or sherry

1 teaspoon soy sauce

1 sweet red pepper or ½ red, ½ yellow pepper, trimmed and sliced lengthwise

4 sheets nori (Japanese seaweed leaves for sushi) (optional)

2 scallions, shredded

1 avocado, peeled, seeded, and sliced lengthwise

½ cup bean sprouts or alfalfa sprouts

½ cup mayonnaise

Rinse the rice well in a colander under cold running water. Place rice in a small pot and cover with water to about 1½ inches above the rice. Add salt and kombu (if used), cover, and bring to a boil; lower the heat and simmer for 40 minutes.

Dissolve the sugar in the rice wine or vinegar and sprinkle over the rice. Mix well, cover the pot, and cook another 5 minutes or more, until the rice is tender and the liquid is absorbed. Cool.

Devein the shrimp by cutting down the back through the shell with a sharp knife but do not remove the shells. Rinse well. Poach for 1 to 2 minutes in boiling water. Remove; cool and shell. Halve the shrimp lengthwise.

Sauté the garlic and pepper pod briefly in butter. Add the crab meat and cook for a few minutes to heat. Add the mirin or sherry and soy sauce, and cook a few minutes more. Remove the pepper pod; cool.

Steam the sweet pepper briefly, just until fork-tender. Cool.

If using nori leaves, they may be roasted by holding them with tongs over an open flame about 1 minute on one side, to release the flavors. This makes them crisp, crumbly, and tasty but harder to handle, so this step may be omitted if desired.

Oil a 9 x 5 x 3-inch loaf pan and line with nori leaves (if used), lapping the leaves over the top of the sides and ends of the pan, to be folded over the finished loaf. Add one-third of the rice; press evenly over the bottom and into the corners. Sprinkle half of the scallions over the rice. Distribute half of the pepper strips and half of the shrimp evenly over the scallions. Add a layer using half of the avocado slices. Spread with half of the mayonnaise, then half of the crab meat mixture. Add another third of the rice and press gently over the layers. Repeat the layers, ending with the final third of the rice. Fold up the ends of the nori leaves firmly over the top of the loaf. Cover with wax paper and set another loaf pan on top to press it down gently. Refrigerate 4 to 6 hours or overnight.

Carefully unmold onto a platter and decorate with your choice of garnishes, such as cut-out vegetable shapes, lemon slices, bean sprouts, and so forth, if desired. Slice with a damp knife, wiped clean between slices.

Creole Chicken Loaf

....

The Creole cuisine of New Orleans combines some of the finest elements of French, Spanish, and African cookery with indigenous American foods. One characteristic flavoring is gumbo filé, a pungent spice derived from sassafras. Serve this loaf with rice.

SERVES 6 TO 8

- 1½ cups chopped onions
- 1 garlic clove, minced
- 1 cup diced celery
- 1 tablespoon unsalted butter
- 1 large egg
- ½ cup heavy cream
- ¼ teaspoon cayenne pepper, or to taste
- 1 teaspoon gumbo filé (optional)
- 1 teaspoon dried oregano
- Salt to taste
- 1½ pounds chicken breast, deboned, skinned, trimmed of fat, and ground
- 1½ cups fine dry bread crumbs
- ½ cup chopped sweet red pepper
- ½ cup chopped green pepper
- 1 small carrot, grated
- 1½ cups chopped fresh tomatoes

Meatloaf

Preheat the oven to 350°F.

Sauté the onions, garlic, and celery briefly in the butter, just until the onions are translucent and the celery is bright green. Cool slightly.

Beat the egg; blend in the cream and seasonings. Add the chicken and bread crumbs, and mix thoroughly. Add the sautéed onions and celery and the peppers, carrot, and tomatoes, and blend gently but thoroughly. Place in an oiled or buttered 9 x 5 x 3-inch loaf pan.

Bake for 45 minutes to 1 hour, until firm and browned.

Corn Belt Loaf

....

A *homey loaf from the Midwest where generations of German, Dutch, and Scandinavian settlers brought with them a taste for such simple, hearty foods.*

SERVES 6 TO 8

1 cup chopped onion
1 garlic clove, minced
1 tablespoon vegetable oil
½ green pepper, chopped
1 large egg
½ teaspoon dried savory
½ teaspoon dried sage, crumbled
Salt and freshly ground black pepper to taste
½ pound ground beef
½ pound ground pork
½ pound sausage meat
1½ cups crumbled cornbread (recipe follows)
1 cup corn kernels (about 1 ear), raw or cooked,
or 1 (10-ounce) package frozen kernels, thawed

Preheat the oven to 350°F.

Sauté the onion and garlic in oil just until the onion is wilted; add the chopped pepper and sauté briefly until bright green. Cool slightly.

Beat the egg and blend in the seasonings. Add the ground beef, pork, and sausage, and mix well. Add the sautéed onion and pepper. Incorporate the cornbread and corn kernels gently but thoroughly. Place in an oiled 9 x 5 x 3-inch loaf pan.

Bake for 45 minutes to 1 hour, until firm.

Variation: To make cornbread pie, preheat the oven to 375°F. Combine all the ingredients above except the crumbled cornbread. Place in a greased 10-inch casserole or baking pan and top with 1½ cups cornbread batter (about one-third of the cornbread recipe below). Bake for 45 minutes to 1 hour, or until the cornbread feels firm to the touch.

Cornbread
....

1 teaspoon baking soda

1 teaspoon salt

¼ teaspoon baking powder

¼ cup sugar

2 cups buttermilk

2 cups cornmeal, preferably stone-ground

½ cup whole wheat flour

¼ cup vegetable oil

Preheat the oven to 350°F.

Butter or oil a 9 x 5 x 3-inch loaf pan and sprinkle with a little cornmeal.

Combine the baking soda, salt, baking powder, and sugar in a food processor (or beat by hand) to break up lumps. Add the buttermilk and blend. Add the cornmeal and flour alternately, mixing well after each addition. Blend in the oil.

Pour into the prepared pan.

Bake for 60 minutes, or until the top feels firm when pressed.

Ethnic
Meatloaf

Meatloaf Stroganoff

. . . .

Like the classic roast beef dish Count Stroganoff created for the Russian tsars in the nineteenth century, this dish combines mushrooms, sour cream, and lean beef. Serve it with lightly buttered noodles or parsleyed new potatoes.

SERVES 6 TO 8

- 1 cup finely chopped onion
- 1 cup mushrooms, stems closely trimmed, thinly sliced
- ¼ cup (½ stick) unsalted butter
- ¼ cup sherry or dry red wine
- 2 large eggs
- 2 pounds ground sirloin
- 2 cups fine dry bread crumbs
- ½ cup finely chopped parsley
- 1 cup sour cream
- ½ teaspoon nutmeg

Preheat the oven to 350°F.

Sauté the onion and mushrooms briefly in butter until the mushrooms release their liquid. Add sherry or wine and continue cooking a few minutes more, until the mushrooms reabsorb the liquid. Cool.

Beat the eggs in a mixing bowl. Add the beef, bread crumbs, parsley, sour cream, and nutmeg; mix well. Add the onion-mushroom mixture and blend. Place the mixture in an oiled or buttered 9 x 5 x 3-inch loaf pan.

Bake for 1 hour, until firm and browned.

Meatloaf Florentine

....

Spinach makes a distinctive addition to a classic Italian meatloaf.

SERVES 4 TO 6

1 pound fresh spinach or one (10-ounce) package frozen
    chopped spinach
¾ pound ground beef
½ pound ground veal or pork (or a combination)
1 cup fine dry bread crumbs
    Salt and freshly ground black pepper to taste
¼ teaspoon freshly grated nutmeg
½ cup finely chopped parsley
¼ cup milk
1 garlic clove, minced
½ cup finely chopped onion
1 tablespoon unsalted butter
2 large eggs, lightly beaten
3 bacon strips

Preheat the oven to 350°F.

Swirl the fresh spinach in a sink full of water to loosen the sand, then rinse individual leaves under running water. Tear off tough stems and discard. Place the spinach with just the water clinging to the leaves in a saucepan. Cover and cook over medium heat for 5 to 8 minutes, turning the leaves over with a wooden spoon after a few minutes. When the spinach is just wilted, remove from the heat, drain in a colander, cool slightly, and press with a wooden spoon to expel moisture. Chop. (If using frozen spinach, follow package directions to cook.)

Mix the meats with the spinach, bread crumbs, and seasonings. Mix in the parsley, milk, and garlic.

Sauté the onion in the butter until wilted and add to the meat mixture. Add the eggs and blend well with your hands. Press into a loaf shape and place in an oiled 9 x 5 x 3-inch baking dish or loaf pan. Cover with the bacon strips.

Bake for 1¼ to 1½ hours, until firm. Let stand 20 minutes and skim off the fat before slicing. Serve with Tomato Sauce (page 96), if desired.

Note: The spinach may be reserved and, before baking, pressed into the center of the loaf as filling, or it can be spread on top of the meat mixture that has been flattened into a rectangle, then rolled up together, jelly-roll style.

Olympian Meatloaf

....

A *heavenly loaf that incorporates classic Greek ingredients.*

SERVES 6 TO 8

½ cup olive oil

2 cups chopped onions

1 cup cooked orzo (Greek pasta) or rice

1 cup raisins

½ pound chestnuts (see Note), chopped

½ cup pine nuts

1½ pounds ground lamb

1 teaspoon ground cloves

½ teaspoon ground cinnamon

   Salt and freshly ground black pepper to taste

1 large egg, lightly beaten

Preheat the oven to 350°F.

Heat the oil in a large skillet and sauté the onion until translucent. Add the orzo or rice, raisins, chestnuts, pine nuts, and lamb. Stir frequently, breaking up any lumps in the meat. Mix in the cloves, cinnamon, salt, and pepper, and remove from the heat. Stir in the egg. Press the mixture into an oiled 9 x 5 x 3-inch loaf pan.

Bake for 45 minutes to 1 hour, until firm and browned.

Note: Canned chestnuts may be purchased at most gourmet shops and many grocery stores. To prepare fresh chestnuts, slash an *X* on the flat side of each nut and either toss the chestnuts with olive oil and bake in one layer on an oiled pan in a 350°F. oven for 30 minutes, or simmer in water to cover about 30 minutes. Cool the chestnuts and peel with a sharp knife. Rub off any of the dry skin that clings to the nuts.

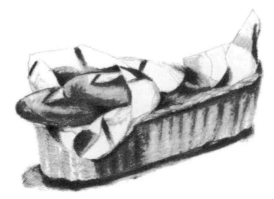

Mama Petrosino's
Meatloaf

....

A *friend who is a minor-league baseball player gave me this family recipe that has been handed down from generation to generation.*

SERVES 6 TO 8

2 pounds ground beef
1 large egg plus 1 egg white
1 garlic clove, minced
  Salt and freshly ground black pepper to taste
½ cup finely chopped parsley
1½ cups fine soft bread crumbs
¼ pound mozzarella cheese

Preheat the oven to 350°F.

Mix together the ground beef, whole egg, garlic, salt, pepper, and parsley. Add the bread crumbs and blend until the mixture feels a little dry. Divide into two balls.

Flatten one ball and place in a buttered or oiled 10-inch baking pan. Slice the mozzarella and cover the meat with the cheese in one layer. Flatten the other ball to fit over the cheese and pinch together the edges of the two portions of meat to seal.

Bake for 1 to 1½ hours, until firm and browned.

Variation: Layer sliced hard-boiled eggs and/or sliced salami with the cheese. Baking time may be increased to 2 hours.

Meatloaf

Mitteleuropean
Meatloaf

....

Horseradish is popular in Hungary, Austria, Germany, and Poland, where the vegetable is stored in root cellars during the winter, ready to enliven the simplest cold-weather dish.

SERVES 4 TO 6

- 3 slices whole wheat bread
- ¼ cup milk
- 1½ pounds ground beef
- ¼ cup horseradish, preferably freshly grated
- 1 tablespoon red wine vinegar
- 2 tablespoons Dijon mustard
- ¼ cup finely chopped onion
- 1½ teaspoons Worcestershire sauce

   Salt and freshly ground black pepper

- 1 large egg, lightly beaten
- 2 tablespoons tomato paste

Preheat the oven to 350°F.

Soak the bread in the milk until soft; drain off any excess milk. Add the bread to the remaining ingredients and combine thoroughly. Place the mixture in an oiled or buttered 9 x 5 x 3-inch loaf pan.

Bake for 45 minutes to 1 hour, until firm and browned. Baste two or three times with the drippings. Let stand 10 minutes before serving.

Lamb and Lentil Loaf

....

A *deeply satisfying and nutritious loaf with origins in the Middle East. Serve with fresh fruit or chutney.*

SERVES 6 TO 8

1 cup dried green lentils

2 cups water

½ teaspoon salt

2 cups chopped fresh greens, such as spinach, beet tops,
    mustard greens, kale, or Swiss chard

3 scallions

1 tablespoon vegetable oil

1 cup fine dry bread crumbs

1 pound ground lamb

2 tart apples such as Granny Smith, finely chopped

2 large eggs

1 tablespoon lemon juice

¼ teaspoon ground cloves

1 teaspoon ground cinnamon

Salt and freshly ground black pepper to taste

Preheat the oven to 350°F.

Cook the lentils in the water and salt for 25 to 30 minutes, or until soft. Drain, pat dry with paper towels, and cool.

Sauté the greens and scallions in the oil just until wilted.

Blend the bread crumbs, lamb, apples, eggs, lemon juice, and seasonings; mix in the lentils and greens until thoroughly blended. Press mixture into an oiled 9 x 5 x 3-inch loaf pan.

Bake for 45 minutes to 1 hour, until firm and browned. Let stand 15 minutes before serving.

Kibbeh

....

A *time-honored delicacy from Lebanon, Kibbeh is a favorite in America's Middle Eastern restaurants. Once tasted, it is never forgotten. Serve with other traditional Middle Eastern dishes such as hummus, stuffed vine leaves, roasted eggplant, and Persian melon.*

SERVES 4 TO 6

2 tablespoons olive oil

1 cup finely chopped onion

2 garlic cloves, minced

1 teaspoon dried basil

½ teaspoon ground cinnamon

¼ teaspoon ground allspice

¾ teaspoon salt

1 pound ground lamb

¼ cup pine nuts

½ cup chopped fresh coriander leaves

½ cup bulgur wheat

1 cup water

Garnish: coriander sprigs and lemon slices

Preheat the oven to 375°F.

Heat the oil in a large skillet. Sauté the onion and garlic until the onion is translucent. Add the basil, cinnamon, allspice, and salt. Mix well. Add half the lamb and cook over medium heat, stirring constantly, until the lamb changes color, about 2 or 3 minutes. Remove from the heat. Stir in the pine nuts and chopped coriander, and let cool.

Cook the bulgur wheat in the water about 15 minutes. Add the remaining lamb and mix thoroughly.

Spread half the lamb-bulgur mixture evenly in an oiled 9 x 5 x 3-inch loaf pan. Cover with the sautéed onion-lamb mixture. Top with the remaining lamb-bulgur mixture. Press down firmly and evenly. Shake the loaf down by striking the pan lightly against the work surface. Precut the loaf into diamond-shaped sections with a sharp knife, cutting through all the layers.

Bake for 40 to 50 minutes, until the edges are browned. Remove from the pan and garnish with coriander sprigs and lemon slices.

Mexican Albóndigas

....

The basic meatloaf of Mexico, this is perhaps at its best in the
northwest areas of Sonora and Jalisco, where some cooks add
chiles chipotles to the sauce for a spicy, smoky flavor.

SERVES 4 TO 6

1 pound ground beef

4 ounces bacon, coarsely chopped

¼ teaspoon ground cumin seeds (optional)

Salt and freshly ground black pepper to taste

1 garlic clove, minced

1 teaspoon finely chopped parsley

1 large egg

1 to 1½ cups Tomato Sauce (page 96)

3 to 4 chiles chipotles (smoked, dried jalapeño peppers; may
   be canned)

¼ cup corn oil

Preheat the oven to 350°F.

Combine the beef, bacon, cumin (if desired), salt, pepper,
garlic, parsley, and egg. Mix with the fingers to blend
thoroughly. Shape into six thick cakes.

Simmer the Tomato Sauce with the chiles chipotles for 10
minutes. Meanwhile, heat the oil in a large skillet and sauté
the cakes until just browned. Place in an ovenproof dish and
cover with the tomato-chile sauce.

Bake for 40 minutes. Serve with rice.

Turkey Pepita Loaf

. . . .

You can adjust the amount of chiles to taste.

SERVES 4 TO 6

    1 cup shelled, unsalted pumpkin seeds
    ¼ teaspoon whole cumin seeds
    2 tablespoons peanut, corn, or other vegetable oil
    1 cup chopped onion
    2 garlic cloves, minced
    1 or 2 fresh chiles serranos or jalapeño peppers, chopped
        finely
    1 cup soft bread crumbs
    1½ pounds ground turkey
    ¼ cup chopped tomato, fresh or canned (without liquid)
    2 large eggs
    1 teaspoon salt
    ½ teaspoon freshly ground black pepper

Preheat the oven to 350°F.

Toast the pumpkin seeds in a stickproof skillet over a
medium flame. Cool slightly and grind together with cumin.

In another skillet, heat the oil over medium heat and
sauté the onions, garlic, and chiles until onion is translucent.
Combine remaining ingredients. Blend in the seeds and
sautéed vegetables. Press into an oiled 9 x 5 x 3-inch loaf pan.

Bake 1 hour until firm. Cool before unmolding.

Game
Meatloaf

Wild Game Meatloaf

. . . .

Wild game meat such as venison, moose, or elk can be sub-stituted for beef in almost any meatloaf recipe. To insure ten-derness, you may want to marinate the meat overnight in red wine with onions, carrots, celery, and herbs before grinding it.

SERVES 4 TO 6

1 large egg

¼ cup tomato paste

1 cup chopped onion

1 garlic clove, minced

1½ pounds game meat (venison, moose, elk, and so forth), ground

¼ pound pork sausage meat

1 cup fine soft bread crumbs, preferably whole wheat

¼ cup chopped parsley

½ teaspoon dried basil

Salt and freshly ground black pepper to taste

Preheat the oven to 350°F.

Beat the egg in a mixing bowl; blend in the tomato paste. Add the remaining ingredients and blend thoroughly. Press into an oiled or buttered 9 x 5 x 3-inch loaf pan.

Bake about 1 hour, until browned and firm.

Variations: Add ¼ cup of sliced green olives stuffed with pi-mientos. Or add 2 tablespoons of Dijon mustard. Or substitute chili sauce or sour cream for part or all of the tomato paste.

Terrine of Rabbit

....

This delectable pâté loaf has a Mediterranean touch. Serve it with artichoke hearts, black olives, figs or other fresh fruit, and crusty bread for lunch or as a first course.

SERVES 8 TO 10

½ cup cognac
1½ cups chopped onions
1 sprig parsley
1 bay leaf
2 cloves
¾ teaspoon dried thyme
4 peppercorns
3 to 4 pounds rabbit (thawed if frozen), boned and cubed
   (reserve the bones)
2 ounces salt pork
2 large eggs
¼ pound foie gras
1¼ cups fine bread crumbs
2 tablespoons olive oil
2 tablespoons red wine vinegar
½ cup chopped celery
¼ cup raisins
¼ cup pine nuts
   Salt and freshly ground black pepper to taste
   Cognac Sauce (recipe follows)

Combine the cognac, 1 cup of the chopped onions, parsley, bay leaf, cloves, ½ teaspoon of the thyme, and peppercorns. Marinate the rabbit in the mixture overnight in the refrigerator, covered.

Preheat the oven to 350°F.

Drain the rabbit, reserving the marinade. Grind the rabbit in a food processor or blender with the salt pork. Remove to a bowl and blend in the eggs, foie gras, bread crumbs, oil, and vinegar. Add the remaining ½ cup of onion, ¼ teaspoon of thyme, celery, raisins, pine nuts, salt and pepper to taste. Press into an oiled 9 x 5 x 3-inch loaf pan. Cover with aluminum foil and set in a larger pan filled with enough hot water to come halfway up the sides of the loaf pan.

Bake 1½ hours, or until firm. Serve with Cognac Sauce.

Cognac Sauce

Cover the rabbit bones with salted water and simmer for at least 2 hours.

Drain and add the reserved cognac marinade. Bring to a boil and reduce to 3 cups.

Strain and adjust the seasonings.

Rabbit Loaf
with Capers

....

A *savory loaf, pungent with capers and anchovies, in the style of southern Italy. The sauce poured on near the end of cooking adds flavor and moisture. Serve with pasta or rice and a green leafy vegetable such as spinach.*

SERVES 4 TO 6

¼ cup red wine vinegar

½ cup dry red wine

1 cup chopped onion

½ cup chopped celery

½ cup chopped carrot

  Salt and freshly ground black pepper to taste

3 to 3½ pounds rabbit (thawed if frozen), boned and cubed

3 tablespoons olive oil

6 anchovies

3 tablespoons drained capers

¼ cup chopped parsley

1 cup fine dry bread crumbs

1 large egg

Combine the vinegar, wine, ½ cup of the chopped onion, celery, carrot, salt, and pepper. Marinate the rabbit in the mixture overnight in the refrigerator.

Preheat the oven to 350°F.

Drain the rabbit and pat dry, reserving the marinade. Grind the rabbit meat in a food processor. Heat the oil and sauté the remaining onion and anchovies briefly, stirring to blend. Combine the rabbit, onion mixture, capers, parsley, bread crumbs, egg, and salt and pepper to taste. Blend thoroughly. Press into an oiled 9 x 5 x 3-inch loaf pan.

Bake for 1 hour.

Meanwhile, bring the reserved marinade to a boil and cook to reduce it by half. Strain and set aside. Pour the sauce over the meatloaf after 1 hour of baking; bake another 30 minutes, until firm.

Game Meatloaf

Smoked Pheasant and Polenta Loaf

....

Based on a classic dish from Tuscany, this loaf imbues an earthy cornmeal pudding with the savory taste of smoked game birds or smoked turkey. Garnish with grapes or other fresh fruit, and serve for lunch or as a first course with extra Parmesan cheese.

SERVES 4 TO 6

9 cups water

2 tablespoons salt

3 cups cornmeal, preferably stone-ground

½ pound fresh mushrooms or 2 ounces dried Italian
    mushrooms, such as boletus, porcini, cepes, and so forth

¼ cup olive oil

¼ cup cubed pancetta or lean ham

½ cup finely chopped onion

½ cup finely chopped celery

½ cup finely chopped carrot

½ cup cubed smoked pheasant or smoked turkey

¼ cup tomato paste

Salt and freshly ground black pepper to taste

Grated Parmesan cheese

Bring the water to a boil in a large, deep pot. Add salt and sprinkle in the cornmeal, stirring continuously with a wooden spoon to prevent lumps. Continue cooking over medium heat, stirring frequently, for 40 to 60 minutes, or until the mixture comes away easily from the sides of the pot. Turn the polenta out onto wax paper and shape into a rectangle about twice the size of the bottom of a 9 x 5 x 3-inch loaf pan. Cool slightly.

Preheat the oven to 350°F.

In a large skillet, sauté the mushrooms in the olive oil until tender. If using dried mushrooms, first soak according to package directions. Remove the mushrooms with a slotted spoon and chop finely. Add the pancetta or ham, onion, celery, and carrot to the pan and sauté briefly. Stir in the pheasant and tomato paste; season the mixture with salt and pepper to taste. Return the mushrooms to the mixture.

Cut the cooled polenta in half and, using two spatulas, remove one half to line the bottom of an oiled 9 x 5 x 3-inch loaf pan. Spread half the pheasant mixture on top and sprinkle with Parmesan cheese. Top with the second half of the polenta and cover with the remaining pheasant mixture; sprinkle with Parmesan cheese.

Bake for 30 to 45 minutes, or until the top is thoroughly browned.

Venison Loaf

....

An excellent way to prepare the tougher cuts of wild venison, this recipe may also be made with meat from farm-raised venison. Serve with wild rice, corn pudding, chestnut puree, wild mushrooms, or fruit compote.

SERVES 4 TO 6

2 cups dry red wine
2 cups chopped onions
1 cup chopped celery
½ cup chopped carrot
1 garlic clove, mashed
1 tablespoon juniper berries
2 pounds boneless venison roast, cubed
¼ pound salt pork
1 cup fine dry bread crumbs, preferably whole wheat
1 tablespoon Dijon mustard
1 large egg
1 teaspoon dried thyme
   Salt and freshly ground black pepper to taste
   Sauce St. Hubert (recipe follows)

Combine the wine with 1 cup of onion and the celery, carrot, garlic, and juniper berries. Marinate the venison in this mixture for at least 4 hours, or overnight if the meat is particularly dry or gamy.

Preheat the oven to 350°F.

Remove the venison from the marinade and pat dry. Process in a food processor with the salt pork until ground. (Or have the butcher grind 2 pounds of tender venison with ¼ pound of salt pork.) Strain the marinade and add ½ cup to the ground venison. Reserve the remaining marinade for sauce. Add the remaining ingredients and blend thoroughly. Press into a buttered or oiled 9 x 5 x 3-inch loaf pan.

Bake for 1 hour or until firm. Serve with Sauce St. Hubert.

Variation: Process the celery, carrot, and garlic from the marinade with the venison and salt pork, if desired. Add ½ cup of chopped fresh parsley.

Sauce St. Hubert
. . . .

MAKES ABOUT 2 CUPS

1 pound venison or beef bones

½ onion

1 small carrot, scraped

1 stalk celery

½ teaspoon dried thyme

1 bay leaf

1 garlic clove

2 teaspoons salt

2 tablespoons all-purpose flour

3 cups water

8 to 10 peppercorns, crushed

1 cup red wine marinade from Venison Loaf, strained

3 tablespoons red currant jelly

Preheat the oven to 450°F.

Place the bones, onion, carrot, celery, thyme, bay leaf, garlic, and salt in a large roasting pan, about 12 x 16 inches. Bake for 1 hour. Sprinkle with the flour and bake a few minutes more.

Add the water and stir, scraping down the sides and bottom of the pan. Transfer the mixture to a 3-quart pot, bring to a boil on top of the stove, and simmer for 2 hours.

Strain the sauce, skim off the fat, and return to the pot. Add the crushed peppercorns and red wine marinade; bring to a boil. Stir in the jelly. Strain and cool slightly before serving.

Meatloaf

Venison Loaf
à l'Orange

....

The light fruit flavoring of this dish belies its richness.

SERVES 4 TO 6

¼ cup (½ stick) unsalted butter, or vegetable oil
1 cup finely chopped onion
1 garlic clove, minced
½ cup chopped celery
¼ pound mushrooms, sliced
1 pound ground lean venison
½ pound ground pork
1 cup soft bread crumbs
  Juice of half an orange
¼ cup heavy cream
2 tablespoons cognac
1 teaspoon salt
  Freshly ground black pepper to taste

Preheat the oven to 350°F.

Heat the butter or oil in a skillet and sauté the onions, garlic, celery, and mushrooms until wilted. Combine the remaining ingredients in a mixing bowl and blend in the sautéed vegetables. Press into an oiled 9 x 5 x 3-inch loaf pan.

Bake 1 hour, until firm. Cool slightly before unmolding.

Meatloaf
Appetizers

Canadian Pâté

....

This North American classic will start off a cocktail party with gusto. Serve it in an earthenware crock with chunks of crusty French bread.

MAKES ABOUT 2 CUPS

⅓ cup raisins
⅓ cup top-quality Canadian whiskey
1 cup plus 2 teaspoons chopped onions
1 cup (2 sticks) unsalted butter
1 large tart apple, cored, peeled, and chopped
1 pound chicken livers
1 teaspoon salt
  Freshly ground black pepper
¼ teaspoon freshly grated nutmeg
2 tablespoons chopped parsley

Soak the raisins in the whiskey for 2 hours or more.

Sauté 1 cup of the onions in the butter. Add the apple and cook 5 minutes. Add the chicken livers, toss them to coat with butter, and sauté about 10 minutes, until the livers lose their pink color. Lower the heat, cover the pan, and simmer 5 minutes more.

Place the liver mixture, raisin-whiskey mixture, and the remaining ingredients in a food processor or blender and blend until smooth. Pack into a buttered mold or loaf pan and chill. Unmold and serve with slices of French bread or crackers.

Vegetable and Veal Terrine

....

Served sliced as a first course or appetizer, this makes an elegant presentation with its brightly colored vegetables complementing the cool green of Watercress Mayonnaise. I like to serve it in the garden with homemade whole wheat crackers and a chilled white zinfandel or rosé wine.

SERVES 6 TO 8

1½ cups chopped onions

1 pound ground veal

¼ pound boiled ham, diced

2 large egg whites

2 tablespoons lemon juice

½ teaspoon dried tarragon, crumbled

Salt and freshly ground white pepper

¾ cup vegetable oil

4 carrots, scraped and quartered lengthwise

10 asparagus spears, with fibrous ends peeled

1 cup green peas, preferably fresh

2 sweet red peppers, or 1 red and 1 yellow, trimmed, seeded, and sliced lengthwise

Watercress Mayonnaise (recipe follows)

Preheat the oven to 400°F.

Blend the onions, veal, ham, and egg whites in a food

processor until smooth (in two batches, if necessary). Blend in the lemon juice, tarragon, salt, and pepper, then the oil. Chill the mixture.

Blanch the carrots, asparagus, peas, and peppers separately in boiling water until barely tender. Test each vegetable with a fork as it cooks; do not overcook. Drain, pat dry, and chill.

Spread a third of the veal mixture evenly over the bottom and sides of an oiled 9 x 5 x 3-inch loaf pan. Spread half of the vegetables over the veal in an attractive color arrangement. Spread another third of the veal over the vegetables. Repeat the layers, ending with a veal layer. Top with a piece of buttered wax paper, buttered side down. Cover tightly with aluminum foil and place the loaf pan in a larger pan filled with enough boiling water to come halfway up the side of the loaf pan.

Place both pans on top of the stove, bring the water back to a boil over high heat, and heat for 5 minutes. Place both pans in the oven and bake for 45 minutes.

Remove the loaf pan and let cool. Cover with plastic wrap. Refrigerate at least 6 hours, preferably overnight. Unmold the loaf carefully onto a platter. Serve with Watercress Mayonnaise.

Watercress Mayonnaise

MAKES 2 CUPS

1½ cups salad oil

1 large egg

1 tablespoon Dijon mustard

1/4 cup finely chopped watercress, tough stems removed
2 teaspoons finely sliced scallions
1 tablespoon lemon juice
1 tablespoon wine vinegar
   Salt and freshly ground black pepper to taste
   Dash of Tabasco

Place 1 tablespoon of the oil with the remaining ingredients in a food processor or blender.

Blending at high speed, very gradually add the remaining oil in a slow, steady stream until the mixture thickens and all the oil is incorporated. Scrape down the sides and blend briefly.

Oriental Meat Rolls

. . . .

This dish makes an unusual and tasty appetizer.

SERVES 4 TO 6

  ¼ pound ground pork

  ¼ cup vegetable oil

  1 garlic clove, minced

  ¼ teaspoon minced fresh ginger

  ¼ cup minced water chestnuts

  3½ ounces (1 can) smoked oysters, drained

  1 pound fresh peas, lightly steamed, or 1 (10-ounce) package
      frozen peas, thawed

  1 tablespoon oyster sauce

  1 teaspoon cornstarch dissolved in 1 tablespoon water

  1 head Boston, leaf, or romaine lettuce

Brown the pork in a wok or deep skillet until it changes
color; remove and keep warm.

Heat the oil in the wok or skillet and stir-fry the garlic
and ginger for 1 minute. Add the water chestnuts and stir-fry
until crisp. Add the oysters, peas, and oyster sauce, and stir-
fry briefly. Blend in the pork and bring to a boil. Add the
cornstarch and stir until the mixture thickens, about 1
minute.

Wash the lettuce leaves and pat dry. Place about 2
tablespoons of the pork mixture in the center of each leaf; fold
in the sides and roll up from the stem end. Serve warm or at
room temperature.

Multinational
Miniloaves

....

Fine fare with cocktails, on the buffet table, or at a picnic.
And they are easy to make. Use your imagination and exper-
tise to create your own variations.

SERVES 8 TO 12

Basic Ingredients for the Following Variations
   3 cups coarsely chopped cooked chicken (preferably white
      meat)
   1½ cups yogurt (approximately)

African Variation
   ¼ cup peanut butter
   1 tablespoon tomato paste
      Dash or 2 of Tabasco
   ½ cup finely ground almonds

Place 1 cup of chicken in a food processor or blender with
the peanut butter, tomato paste, Tabasco, and 2 tablespoons of
yogurt. Process, scraping down the sides and adding more
yogurt if necessary to produce a thick paste. Roll the mixture
into 1½-inch balls; roll the balls in the ground almonds. Chill
thoroughly on wax paper.

Indian Variation

 1 teaspoon curry powder

 ½ teaspoon cinnamon

 2 tablespoons chutney, minced

 ¼ cup confectioners' sugar

Place 1 cup of chicken in a food processor or blender with the curry, cinnamon, and ½ cup of yogurt. Process until formed into a paste; add the chutney and process briefly to mix. Roll into 1½-inch balls; roll the balls in the confectioners' sugar. Chill on wax paper.

Mexican Variation

 ½ cup grated cheddar cheese

 ·1 teaspoon chili powder

 ¼ teaspoon dried oregano

 ½ teaspoon garlic powder

   Dash or 2 of Tabasco, or to taste

 ¼ cup finely minced parsley

Place 1 cup of chicken in a food processor or blender with the cheddar cheese, ½ cup of yogurt, chili powder, oregano, garlic powder, and Tabasco. Process until the mixture forms a paste. Roll into 1½-inch balls; roll the balls in the minced parsley. Chill on wax paper.

To serve, arrange the miniloaves in three separate sections on a platter lined with lettuce. Skewer the balls with toothpicks (color-keyed for each variation) if desired.

Mediterranean Loaf

....

A taste of coastal Italy, where tuna and anchovies are traditional favorites and the olive groves provide the earthy-flavored oil for such simple peasant dishes. Try it as a savory appetizer at your next outdoor meal.

SERVES 4 TO 6

1 pound fresh spinach or 1 (10-ounce) package frozen whole
   spinach, thawed
1 (3½-ounce) can tuna in olive oil, preferably Italian
4 anchovies
1 slice good-quality white bread, untrimmed
½ cup milk
2 large eggs, lightly beaten
½ cup freshly grated Parmesan cheese or half Parmesan, half
   Romano
½ teaspoon dried oregano
   Salt and freshly ground black pepper to taste
2 tablespoons lemon juice

Garnish: lemon slices

If using fresh spinach, break off the tough stems and rinse the leaves in a pot or sink full of water. Rinse again under running water. Put the leaves in a large pot without draining; cover and cook over low heat for about 8 minutes, until tender, stirring and turning the leaves over with a wooden spoon at least once. Drain and let cool slightly.

Extract excess moisture by pressing the leaves against the sides of a colander with a wooden spoon. (If using frozen spinach, follow the package directions for cooking.) Chop the spinach finely.

Drain the tuna of excess oil and chop it finely with the anchovies. Mix with the spinach in a bowl.

Soak the bread in the milk for 5 to 10 minutes. Squeeze out the excess milk gently and add the bread to the tuna mixture. Add the eggs, cheese, oregano, salt, pepper, and lemon juice.

Pat the mixture into a roll about 3 inches in diameter. Wrap in several layers of cheesecloth or roll up in a clean tea towel or other cloth; tie at each end. Place the roll in a flame-proof baking dish in which it fits closely and cover it with boiling water. Cover the dish with a lid. Bring to a boil over high heat, then lower the heat and simmer for 30 minutes. (For ease of handling the cooked roll, let the ends of the cloth stick out of the pot; wet them and fold over the lid to prevent them from burning.)

Remove the roll from the dish by lifting the ends of the cloth. Cool slightly; remove from the cloth and cool completely. Cut the roll into slices and garnish with lemon slices.

Variation: Blend all ingredients as directed except the spinach. Roll the tuna mixture out into a rectangle about 10 inches long. Spread with a layer of spinach and roll up jelly-roll style; or place the spinach in a strip down the center and wrap the tuna mixture around it. Roll in a cloth and proceed as above.

Ham and
Mushroom Pâté

....

This deceptively simple appetizer is raised to gourmet status
when served with toasted slices of French bread.

SERVES 4 TO 6

1 pound fresh mushrooms
1 cup coarsely chopped onion
1 large egg
¼ cup sour cream
½ teaspoon dried tarragon
¼ teaspoon nutmeg
Salt and freshly ground black pepper to taste
1½ pounds boiled or baked ham, ground or finely minced
½ cup chopped parsley
¼ cup (½ stick) unsalted butter, melted (optional)

Preheat the oven to 350°F.

Wash and trim the mushrooms, and chop coarsely. Place
in a food processor or blender and briefly blend with the
onion, egg, sour cream, tarragon, nutmeg, salt, and pepper.
Add the ham and half the parsley, and process just enough to
blend.

Press the mixture into a well-buttered 9 x 5 x 3-inch loaf
pan and cover with foil. Place the loaf pan in a larger pan
filled with enough boiling water to come halfway up the sides
of the pan.

Bake for 1 to 1½ hours. Cool.

Unmold the loaf onto a serving platter. Drizzle the melted butter over the loaf, if desired, and sprinkle with the remaining parsley. Refrigerate until ready to serve.

Terrine Garni

....

A rich *pâté decorated in the classic French style, this loaf demands the patience and painstaking attention to detail required by yesterday's cuisine. But the oohs and aahs it produces make it worth the effort.*

SERVES 6 TO 8

Pâté

½ pound chopped calves' or chicken livers

½ cup chopped onion

2 anchovies

2 tablespoons cognac

3 tablespoons fine dry bread crumbs

   Salt and freshly ground black pepper to taste

2 large eggs

1 cup heavy cream

¼ teaspoon nutmeg

½ teaspoon dried tarragon, crumbled

2 tablespoons (¼ stick) unsalted butter, melted

Tomato Aspic

3 cups chicken stock

1 cup tomato paste

   Salt and freshly ground black pepper to taste

1 teaspoon sugar

2 egg shells, crushed

1 large egg, lightly beaten

4 tablespoons (4 envelopes) unflavored gelatin

2 tablespoons brandy

Garnish: sliced truffles, olives, blanched red peppers, carrot slices, and hard-boiled eggs, cut into various shapes as desired, and parsley sprigs

Preheat the oven to 350°F.

Combine the livers, onion, anchovies, and cognac in a food processor or blender. Add the bread crumbs, salt, pepper, and eggs, and continue blending until smooth. Add the cream while processing; add the nutmeg, tarragon, and butter.

Butter well a 1-quart loaf pan or mold and chill. Line the bottom of the pan with a piece of wax paper cut to the same size. Butter the paper. Pour the liver mixture into the pan. Place another piece of wax paper, cut to fit the top of the pan, on top of the liver mixture. Place the pan in a larger pan filled with enough boiling water to come halfway up the sides.

Bake for 35 to 40 minutes, or until the top of the loaf springs back lightly to the touch. Let stand until cool, then refrigerate until chilled and firm.

Unmold the loaf onto a platter, discard the wax paper, and return the pâté to the refrigerator.

Wash and dry the pan, and chill it in the freezer.

Meanwhile, make the aspic. Combine all the ingredients except the gelatin, brandy, and garnishes. Heat slowly to a boil. Add the gelatin and dissolve.

Remove from the heat and stir in the brandy. Strain the mixture through cheesecloth. Refrigerate until chilled but still liquid.

Pour ½ cup of liquid aspic into the chilled loaf pan and

roll carefully to coat the sides and bottom. Pour off the excess aspic. Chill the pan. Repeat this process about 6 times, chilling after each layer of aspic, then add about ½ inch of aspic to the bottom of the mold and chill to set. (You may wish to reheat the aspic if it becomes too firm while you are assembling the loaf.)

Dip the garnishes in the remaining liquid aspic and arrange them attractively over the bottom of the pan. Return the pâté to the pan, easing it gently into place over the garnishes. Fill in any spaces between the pâté and the sides of the pan with more liquid aspic and cover the top with aspic. Chill several hours until firmly set. Unmold onto a platter and garnish with sprigs of parsley as desired.

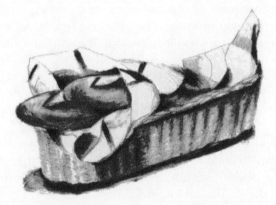

Light Chicken
Liver Pâté

....

This savory low-calorie pâté is festive enough for company, yet a boon for dieters.

MAKES ABOUT 3 CUPS

1 pound chicken livers
1 hard-boiled egg
1 cup chopped onion
½ cup mayonnaise
1 tablespoon fresh lemon juice
1 tablespoon soy sauce
1 tablespoon cognac
½ teaspoon crumbled dried sage
½ teaspoon salt
Freshly ground black pepper to taste

Cook the livers in a nonstick skillet over medium heat until they lose their pink color.

Combine with the remaining ingredients in a food processor or blender and process until smooth.

Pack mixture into a crock and refrigerate for several hours or overnight. Serve with French bread or crackers.

Meatloaf from Leftovers

Friday Night Meatloaf

....

A *memorable meatloaf can result from years of culinary experience or from the accumulation of last week's leftovers. (My mother-in-law calls the latter End-of-the-Week Cookery.)*

You can usually count on having leftovers from holiday dinners, parties, buffets, and Chinese take-out. These are popular with noshers, but you may have a few left at the end of the week. Other leftovers aren't so popular, which is probably why they were left over. The cauliflower the kids wouldn't eat, the elegant sweetbread dish you slaved over and everyone hated —these are grist for the meatloaf mill.

There's only one problem with a creative meatloaf: If your family adores it, they may ask you to make it again—and you may never have the same set of leftovers the next time around.

On Friday, take stock of your leftovers and use your imagination. The basic "food groups" of a meatloaf are meat, bread, binding, moistener, and flavorings. Decide which of these groups your leftovers belong to, and follow this basic recipe.

SERVES 6

Meat:	2 pounds or 3 cups meat
Bread:	1 cup bread crumbs
Binding:	1 egg
Moistener:	½ cup liquid, such as milk, stock, wine, or water
Flavorings:	Herbs, spices, salt, and pepper to taste

Mix, shape into a loaf, or press into a prepared loaf pan, and bake in a preheated 350°F. oven for 45 minutes to 1 hour.

Some Tips: *If you have a leftover hamburger, crumble it and mix it with enough raw ground meat to make 2 pounds. Add a little extra liquid to compensate for any that has already been cooked out of the hamburger.*

Leftover cooked rice, pasta, or mashed potatoes can be substituted for part of the bread. Include about ¼ cup of fine bread crumbs to ensure a firm texture in the finished loaf.

Casseroles and stews may count for several of a meatloaf's food groups. Macaroni and cheese is both meat and bread, for instance. Beef stew is meat and liquid. And pizza can be both bread and flavorings. (Crumble it in the food processor or mince it.)

If you're using leftover vegetables or vegetable dishes, drain them thoroughly and also use the drained liquid to moisten the loaf. Mix the vegetables into the loaf or make a center filling of them, or use them to create a roulade or jelly-roll–type loaf.

If your mixture is a bit heavy on solid ingredients, add a second egg to bind it all together.

Soups of all kinds make excellent moisteners.

As for flavoring, the rule of thumb when using leftovers is to combine flavors carefully. Tuna noodle casserole may not mix very well with chili, though it would be fine with plain ground veal. The flavor of broiled salmon could get lost if paired with cheddar cheese or Mexican salsa. Add Italian herbs to a pizza loaf.

Use seasonings with caution. Some ingredients may provide all the flavoring necessary. Experience will teach you how far certain flavors extend in combination with others.

Applesauce Loaf

. . . .

Clean out the bottoms of all those near-empty applesauce jars in the refrigerator for use in this tasty loaf. You may substitute ½ cup of apple butter for the cup of applesauce, and add approximately ¼ cup of water or milk.

SERVES 6 TO 8

2 pounds ground beef

1 cup applesauce (preferably sugarless)

½ cup chopped onion

½ cup chopped green pepper

1 garlic clove, minced

½ cup raisins

1 cup bread crumbs, preferably whole wheat

1 large egg

¼ teaspoon allspice

Salt and freshly ground black pepper to taste

Preheat the oven to 350°F.

Combine all the ingredients thoroughly. Press into an oiled or buttered 9 x 5 x 3-inch loaf pan.

Bake for 1¼ hours, until browned and firm.

Southern Sweet Potato Loaf

....

Don't throw away those leftover sweet potatoes. They will add a delicate, almost creamy texture to this unusual Southern-style loaf. Use up leftover vegetables, too, in place of the celery and okra.

SERVES 6 TO 8

1 tablespoon vegetable oil

2 garlic cloves, minced

1 cup chopped onion

1 cup chopped celery

1 cup trimmed and thinly sliced okra

2 pounds boneless, skinless chicken or turkey breast, trimmed
 of fat and cartilage and cubed

1 large egg, beaten

1 cup heavy cream or sour cream

2 cups cooked mashed sweet potato

3 tablespoons tomato paste

1 cup chopped sweet red pepper

1 cup chopped fresh tomato

1 teaspoon dried oregano

1 teaspoon dried thyme

 Tabasco and/or hot red pepper to taste

 Salt to taste

Meatloaf

Preheat the oven to 350°F.

Heat the oil in a skillet; sauté the garlic, onion, and celery just until the onion is translucent and the celery is bright green. Add the okra; cook a few minutes more. Cool slightly. (Omit this step if using precooked vegetables.)

Process the chicken or turkey with the egg, cream, sweet potato, and tomato paste in a food processor or blender until smooth. (It may be necessary to process them in two batches).

Thoroughly blend the sautéed vegetables and the remaining ingredients with the chicken or turkey mixture. Press into an oiled or buttered 9 x 5 x 3-inch loaf pan.

Bake for 1 hour. Let the loaf stand 15 minutes before serving. Garnish with baby okra, parboiled or lightly steamed, if desired.

Ham and Eggs Loaf

....

Kids love this loaf, which is a lovely shade of green with reddish bits of ham. It's a great way to get everyone to eat greens and to use up leftover hard-boiled eggs or ham. Spinach or beet greens may be substituted for Swiss chard.

SERVES 4 TO 6

1 pound fresh Swiss chard

2 large eggs

½ cup milk

2 tablespoons vegetable oil or unsalted butter

1 cup fine dry bread crumbs, preferably whole wheat

Salt and freshly ground black pepper to taste

½ pound ham, cubed

Garnish: 1 or 2 large hard-boiled eggs, sliced

Preheat the oven to 375°F.

Trim the stems of the Swiss chard and rinse the leaves well. Steam in a vegetable steamer or simmer in a small amount of boiling water until the stems are just tender, about 10 minutes. Drain well and chop into ½-inch shreds.

Combine the eggs, milk, oil or butter, bread crumbs, salt, and pepper, and mix well. Add the chard and ham, and combine thoroughly.

Place the mixture in a buttered 9 x 5 x 3-inch loaf pan, cover with foil, and set it in a larger pan filled with enough boiling water to come halfway up the sides of the loaf pan.

Bake for 25 minutes, or until firm. Unmold the loaf and garnish with hard-boiled egg slices.

Variation: Prepare the mixture as above. Line a 12-inch pie or quiche pan with pie dough (frozen puff pastry may be used) and pour the chard mixture over the dough. Bake as above and garnish with hard-boiled egg slices.

Thanksgiving
Turkey Loaf

....

You'll give thanks for leftover turkey when you taste this loaf. You may even plan a larger turkey for next year to make sure you have enough leftovers! Serve it with baked sweet potatoes and cranberry sauce or, for a change of pace, buttered noodles and asparagus.

SERVES 4 TO 6

1½ pounds cooked turkey, preferably white meat, ground
  2 cups leftover cooked stuffing (any standard recipe)
  2 large eggs, lightly beaten
  ½ cup fine soft bread crumbs
  ½ cup turkey gravy or heavy cream, or a mixture of both
  ½ cup minced shallots
  1 teaspoon dried thyme, sage, savory, or poultry seasoning,
      whichever is compatible with the stuffing flavoring;
      poultry seasoning is usual in most standard stuffing
      recipes
  Salt and freshly ground black pepper to taste

Preheat the oven to 350°F.

Blend all ingredients thoroughly. If the stuffing is dry (for example, if it was baked outside the turkey), you may need to add more cream or gravy.

Press the mixture into an oiled or buttered 9 x 5 x 3-inch loaf pan.

Bake for 45 minutes to 1 hour, until brown and firm.

Variation: *For Curried Turkey Loaf,* omit thyme or other herbs. Add 1 teaspoon curry powder, ¼ teaspoon powdered ginger, and 1 minced garlic clove. You may replace the gravy or sour cream with the juice of one lemon, and add ½ cup grated coconut (unsweetened) if desired. Serve the loaf with rice (perhaps Basmati rice), accompanied by chutney, chopped peanuts, fresh coriander leaves, raisins, and/or your choice of hot sauce.

Sauces

Sorrel Sauce

....

This colorful sauce is a perfect foil for delicate chicken or veal meatloaves. It is also excellent with other chicken dishes and with pork or seafood. Sorrel can usually be found in season during the spring.

MAKES ABOUT 1½ CUPS

¾ cup chicken stock
1½ cups chopped fresh sorrel leaves
2 tablespoons (¼ stick) unsalted butter
1½ tablespoons flour
½ cup heavy cream
Juice of half a lemon
Salt and freshly ground black pepper to taste

Bring the stock to a boil and simmer the sorrel in it for 5 minutes. Process in a food processor or blender until smooth.

Melt the butter in a saucepan over medium heat until it foams. Add the flour, stirring briskly with a whisk, and cook a few minutes, stirring. Blend in the sorrel, then the cream and lemon juice. Season to taste with salt and pepper.

Tomato Sauce

....

Serve this rich, full-bodied sauce with any beef, pork, or lamb loaf. It's obviously the right choice with such Italian-style meatloaves as Giacomo's, Florentine, and Mama Petrosino's, and with Mexican Albóndigas. It makes a gentle foil for a fiery Creole Chicken or Tex-Mex loaf, too. The fine, fresh flavor of this versatile sauce will complement Corn Belt Loaf and brighten up your Friday Night Meatloaf. Spread it on top of a loaf before cooking to help retain moisture, or ensure a juicy loaf by basting it with the sauce 15 minutes before the loaf is finished. If a meatloaf turns out dry or dull, spoon warm sauce over the slices.

MAKES 3 TO 4 CUPS

1 pound ripe tomatoes (plum tomatoes or whatever variety is
     in season)
1 onion, coarsely chopped
1 stalk celery, coarsely chopped
1 carrot, scraped and coarsely chopped
2 garlic cloves, chopped
1 bay leaf
½ teaspoon dried oregano
½ teaspoon basil
    Salt and freshly ground black pepper to taste

Drop the tomatoes into boiling water for about 30 seconds to loosen the skins. Remove with a slotted spoon, cool briefly in cold water, and pull off the skins. (Or skip this step if you don't mind bits of peel in the finished sauce.) Core and chop the tomatoes coarsely; remove the seeds if you wish.

In a heavy saucepan, cook the tomatoes over medium heat, uncovered, stirring frequently, until they become soft and juicy. Add the remaining ingredients and cook, stirring, about 30 minutes more.

Remove the bay leaf and process the mixture in a food processor or blender until smooth. Return the sauce to the saucepan and cook, uncovered, to reduce it to the desired thickness, about 15 minutes.

Variations: Omit the celery and/or carrot, or remove them before processing.

Vary the flavor by using tarragon, sage, savory, anise seeds, celery seeds, thyme, Dijon mustard, lemon juice, or wine vinegar.

Add ½ cup of yogurt to the sauce after removing it from the heat for a delicate, creamy sauce.

Mushroom Sauce

....

This is a rich, savory sauce that will dress up the humblest meatloaf. Remember, though, that a sauce should be a partner to a meatloaf, and that while neither should overpower the other, the meatloaf is the hero in this partnership. So don't gussy up an already full-flavored loaf with a sauce like this one.

MAKES ABOUT 2 CUPS

2 garlic cloves, finely minced

¼ cup (½ stick) unsalted butter or vegetable oil, or a combination of both

1 pound mushrooms, trimmed and sliced (about 4 cups)

3 tablespoons all-purpose flour

1 large egg

1 cup milk or half-and-half

1 tablespoon lemon juice

¼ teaspoon dried thyme

Salt and freshly ground white pepper to taste

Freshly grated nutmeg to taste

Sauté the garlic in 1 tablespoon of the butter or oil. Add the mushrooms and cook briefly, until they begin giving up their liquid. Remove the mushrooms and reserve.

Heat the remaining butter or oil over medium heat until the butter foams or the oil is hot. Add the flour and stir briskly with a wire whisk until completely combined;

continue cooking about 5 minutes more.

Beat the egg with the milk or half-and-half. Add slowly to the butter mixture, whisking briskly, until the mixture begins to thicken. Add the lemon juice slowly, then add the thyme, salt, and pepper.

Return the mushrooms to the sauce and heat, stirring thoroughly to blend in the mushroom liquid. Stir in the nutmeg.

Variation: Substitute 2 tablespoons of red wine or sherry for the lemon juice. Add before the egg and milk, and bring to a boil; boil for 30 seconds. Proceed as above.

Salsa Cruda

....

A quick and easy way to zip up any meatloaf, this refreshing Mexican sauce is an excellent partner for the Tex-Mex or Creole Chicken loaf. It is traditionally prepared just minutes before serving. Vary the spiciness by using more or less jalapeño pepper.

MAKES ABOUT 1½ CUPS

1 medium tomato (about ½ pound), minced
3 scallions, minced
½ cup minced green pepper
2 to 4 tablespoons jalapeño pepper (or to taste), finely minced
¼ cup lime juice
½ teaspoon salt

Blend all ingredients thoroughly. Serve promptly.

Watercress Sauce

....

Delicate *enough for the subtlest meatloaf, with the zest of watercress for added interest. Serve with the Pain de Poule or with any simple chicken, turkey, or veal loaf.*

MAKES ABOUT 3 CUPS

1 small bunch watercress
3 tablespoons unsalted butter
3 tablespoons flour
2½ cups chicken or veal stock
½ cup heavy cream
   Salt and freshly ground black pepper to taste

Remove and discard the stems from the watercress. Blanch the watercress for about 30 seconds in boiling water. Drain, dry with paper towels, and chop finely.

Heat the butter in a saucepan over medium heat until it foams. Add the flour, stirring briskly with a whisk. Cook a few minutes. Add the stock slowly, whisking briskly. Cook about 15 minutes, stirring frequently.

Add the cream slowly, stirring continuously. Add the salt and pepper. Simmer another 15 minutes, stirring occasionally. Stir in the watercress.

Raisin Sauce

....

A *rich, fruity sauce like this is an excellent accompaniment to beef, ham, and pork meatloaves.*

MAKES ABOUT 3 CUPS

1 cup raisins
1 cup water
¾ cup sherry
1 stick cinnamon
¼ cup dark brown sugar, packed
1½ tablespoons cornstarch
½ teaspoon Dijon mustard
½ teaspoon salt
¼ teaspoon cloves
1 tablespoon unsalted butter
1 tablespoon vinegar

Simmer the raisins in the water and sherry with the cinnamon stick for 5 minutes.

Mix the brown sugar, cornstarch, mustard, salt, and cloves, and add to the raisin mixture. Bring to a boil and simmer for 15 minutes.

Remove the sauce from the heat. Discard the cinnamon stick. Stir in the butter and vinegar.

Figgy Sauce

....

An unusual sauce that adds an exotic flavor to the most mundane meatloaf. The fruit flavoring lends lushness to beef, veal, lamb, and pork dishes. Kids of all ages love this sauce so much you may find them asking for more before they've even started on their meatloaf!

MAKES ABOUT 2 CUPS

- 1½ teaspoons cornstarch
- 2 tablespoons lemon juice
- 1½ cups unsweetened grape juice
  Salt to taste
- 1 cup minced dried figs
  Honey to taste (optional)

Combine the cornstarch and lemon juice in a saucepan. Gradually stir in the grape juice and salt to taste. Bring the mixture to a boil, stirring constantly, then simmer 5 minutes.

Stir in the minced figs. Simmer for 1 minute more. Remove from the heat and add honey to taste, if desired. Let the sauce stand 15 minutes to soften the figs.

Index

....